Original title:
Stolen Moments

Copyright © 2024 Swan Charm
All rights reserved.

Author: Mirell Mesipuu
ISBN HARDBACK: 978-9908-1-2716-3
ISBN PAPERBACK: 978-9908-1-2717-0
ISBN EBOOK: 978-9908-1-2718-7

The Art of Fading

In shadows deep where secrets lie,
Whispers fade, like a soft sigh.
The colors dim, the echoes cease,
Time dances on, finding peace.

Each moment breaks, a fragile thread,
As memories drift, the heart is led.
A gentle fade, a quiet end,
The art of letting go, my friend.

Remnants of a Soft Touch

In tender light, your fingers trace,
A world of dreams, a warm embrace.
Each lingering kiss, a fleeting glow,
Remnants of love, like melted snow.

Silent whispers in the night,
Ghostly shadows take their flight.
Yet in the heart, they softly stay,
The touch of you, won't fade away.

The Lost Diary's Pages

In a dusty drawer, the pages lie,
Stories woven, where time drifts by.
Ink long dried, the words unclear,
Yet feelings surge, still held so dear.

Each heartbeat sings, a silent call,
Memories cling, as shadows fall.
A life once lived, a truth profound,
In lost pages, love is found.

Interludes of Joy

In laughter's burst, we find our way,
Moments bright, like a sunlit day.
Life's quick dance, a fleeting glance,
Interludes sweet, the heart does prance.

A song of hope in every cheer,
Whispers of joy that draw us near.
In tiny bliss, life's grande tour,
Interludes of joy, forever pure.

Breaths Between the Beats

In the silence, whispers dwell,
Moments quiet, stories tell.
Hearts in rhythm, soft and true,
Each breath taken, me and you.

Under stars, we chase the light,
Echoed dreams in the night.
Threads of time, tightly spun,
Every second, just begun.

Softly drifting, like the breeze,
Memories dance among the trees.
Time may pause, yet we remain,
In this world, a sweet refrain.

Vanishing Footprints

Upon the shore, the tides will shift,
Leaving marks, a fleeting gift.
Waves will wash them, fade away,
But memories in hearts will stay.

Pedals crushed 'neath summer's glow,
Each step forward, ebb and flow.
In the sand, our stories thread,
Yet with the tide, they soon are shed.

Chasing shadows, dusk will fall,
Whispers rising, nature's call.
Footprints linger for a time,
Before they're lost, a silent rhyme.

When Time Paused

In a moment, stillness found,
Time suspended, no more sound.
Eyes that meet, the world erased,
Lost in wonder, hearts embraced.

Golden light through rustling leaves,
Nature breathes in gentle eves.
Hands held tight, we drift away,
In this space, we'll always stay.

Memories dance in twilight's hue,
Every glance, a promise new.
When the clock forgets to chime,
We are living, pure sublime.

The Locket of Lost Days

In the locket, secrets hide,
This treasure chest, my heart's guide.
Rusty keys and whispers deep,
Unraveled tales, joy and weep.

Pages turn in faded books,
Each story carries loving looks.
Time unbound, moments soared,
In precious fragments, life adored.

Through every tear, a lesson learned,
In the fires of passion burned.
Hold it close, the locket sways,
Guarding dreams of lost days.

The Sound of Goodbye

A soft whisper fills the air,
Echoes linger in despair.
Fading steps on a dusty road,
Memories fade, a heavy load.

Eyes close tight, a final glance,
Each heartbeat, a fleeting chance.
Words unsaid cling to the night,
Shadows dance in dimming light.

Once so bright, now turned to gray,
Time slips slowly, fades away.
In the stillness, silence grows,
The sound of goodbye, softly flows.

Windows to Yesterday

Through the panes of dusk and dawn,
Fragments of a time now gone.
Images in the glass reflect,
Moments past we still protect.

Faded laughter, silent screams,
Caught within our waking dreams.
Each glance back, a bittersweet,
A dance of time, a hidden beat.

Footsteps echo, soft and slow,
Where the sun used to glow.
Windows framed in soft regret,
Yesterday, a silhouette.

Fragments of a Daydream

In the corners of my mind,
Fragments of the dreams I find.
Whispers dancing on my skin,
A world where fantasies begin.

Colors blend in soft embrace,
Time stands still in this sacred space.
Chasing shadows, lost in flight,
Daydreams spark in endless night.

Cascading thoughts like gentle rain,
Washing away the weight of pain.
Scattered pieces find their place,
Fragments of a dream I trace.

In the Quiet of Time

In the quiet, silence hums,
Softly calling, gently drums.
Moments weave a tapestry,
In the stillness, we are free.

Carefree whispers fill the air,
Memories linger everywhere.
Every pause, a breath of peace,
As the world begins to cease.

Stars align in velvet skies,
While dreams bloom and spirits rise.
In the calm, we find our rhyme,
Rhythm flows in the quiet of time.

The Heartbeat Between Moments

In the stillness of the night,
A pulse brews soft and light,
Time slows, then starts anew,
In breaths both deep and true.

Silence dances in the air,
Embracing hearts laid bare,
Each tick, a tender sigh,
As fleeting moments fly.

Shadows weave in twilight's glow,
With secrets only lovers know,
The world fades into a blur,
In whispers, nothing stirs.

Yet in that space, we feel alive,
Where echoes of our dreams arrive,
The heartbeat plays its gentle song,
In between where we belong.

A symphony of heartbeats caught,
In memories that time forgot,
Here we linger, here we stay,
Between the night and break of day.

Fleeting Whispers

Beneath the sky's vast dome,
Soft whispers call us home,
Through fields where shadows chase,
Memories find their place.

Moments slip like grains of sand,
In a child's gentle hand,
Each laugh, each echo fades,
In the twilight glades.

Time dances on the breeze,
With secrets held in trees,
Fleeting whispers in the night,
Holding dreams so tight.

Yet in the hush, we find our way,
Where hearts and melodies play,
Moments stretching, bending light,
Crafting shadows out of sight.

As dawn's embrace pulls us near,
Every whisper turns to fear,
Loss is part of love's sweet art,
Fleeting echoes, cherish heart.

The Time Thief

He creeps through hours, silent, sly,
The time thief never says goodbye,
With every laugh, a moment lost,
In the memoirs, we count the cost.

Each second stolen, each kiss held tight,
Transformed by dreams into the night,
He sways the pendulum with his charm,
Unaware of the hearts he'll harm.

Tick tock, the clock laments,
In memories, the heart repents,
For every joy, a tear will show,
As shadows dance across the flow.

Yet in the grasp of fleeting days,
Life finds beauty in its ways,
The time thief steals, but leaves behind,
Treasures woven in our mind.

So let the moments come and go,
In stolen hours, love will grow,
We'll chase the shadows, we will fight,
While hearts burn bright in endless light.

Echoes of Yesterday

In the corridors of time,
Whispers linger, softly prime,
Echoes dance like dust in sun,
Reminders of the battles won.

Memories strung like pearls on thread,
Voices call from paths we tread,
Each snapshot holds a story fair,
In laughter's glow, we find our share.

Yet ghosts of dreams may haunt the dawn,
As we ponder what is gone,
The laughter fades, the silence grows,
In toil, the heart just knows.

But amidst the echoes, solace lies,
In every smile, in every sigh,
Past moments weave the tapestry,
Of who we are, of love's decree.

So hold the echoes close and tight,
For in them, we find our light,
Yesterday's dance forever stays,
In the heart of endless days.

Whispers of Time

In the still of night, secrets call,
Shadows dance on the old brick wall.
Moments slip through fingers like sand,
Traveling so fast, like a silent hand.

Echoes linger in the cool, soft air,
Memories stitched with delicate care.
Fleeting tales of joy and woe,
Whispers of time, so gentle and slow.

Beneath the stars, dreams entwine,
Fading softly, a thread divine.
Each heartbeat marks the passing days,
In the hush, the heart's maze plays.

As dawn unfolds its golden guise,
We chase the sun, where hope lies.
Yet in the dusk, our voices blend,
A bittersweet song that knows no end.

Fleeting Fragments of Light

Sunrise paints the world anew,
A canvas brushed with every hue.
Moments glow, then quickly fade,
In the dance of light, our dreams are laid.

Fireflies twinkle in the dark,
Whispers of hope, a tiny spark.
The night hums a lullaby sweet,
Guiding us on with silent feet.

Shadows lengthen as day departs,
Fragments of light play in our hearts.
Capturing time in a fleeting grasp,
Together we write, our stories clasp.

In the twilight, we find our peace,
Embracing moments that never cease.
Fleeting fragments disappear fast,
Yet in their glow, the memories last.

The Quiet Thief

In the silence, a shadow creeps,
Stealing dreams and tangled sleeps.
The night, a cloak of secrets bold,
Whispers tales that should be told.

Time, the thief in the softest guise,
Snatches moments from hopeful ties.
With gentle hands, it lifts away,
All the colors of yesterday.

Each heartbeat fades into night's embrace,
Like a fleeting smile on a stranger's face.
Yet in loss, the heart grows wise,
Finding truths beneath the skies.

The quiet thief dances in the breeze,
Mending hearts with tender ease.
In the stillness, we find our way,
Learning to cherish each passing day.

Echoes of the Unseen

In the corners where shadows blend,
Echoes of whispers seem to send.
Stories untold linger on the brink,
Leaving thoughts for us to think.

Silent moments stretch so wide,
Holding secrets we wish to hide.
The wind carries tales through the trees,
Rustling softly like forgotten leaves.

In daylight's glow and nighttime's chill,
Echoes of the unheard instill.
Glimmers of a world we barely see,
The hidden paths that set us free.

Beneath the surface, magic swirls,
Unseen wonders in a dance unfurls.
We search for meaning, deep in the night,
Finding comfort in the purest light.

Shadows in a Timeless Dance

In twilight's gentle grasp they sway,
Whispers of dreams from yesterday.
Figures carved in starlit hue,
Shadows that play, ever so true.

They twirl beneath the silver moon,
Hearts entwined in a silent tune.
Each step echoes through the years,
A ballet painted by joy and tears.

Ghostly forms in the garden's light,
Fleeting glimpses of joyful night.
They merge and part like falling leaves,
In the memories that the heart weaves.

As dawn approaches, they fade away,
Carried by the light of day.
Yet in the echoes, they still prance,
Timeless spirits in a dance.

Forever bound to the night's embrace,
In every corner, we find their trace.
Shadows whisper what time cannot,
In every moment, they are caught.

Silhouettes of Forgotten Laughter

In corners of rooms where joy once bloomed,
Silhouettes linger, in shadows consumed.
Echoes of laughter, soft as a sigh,
Painting the air, where memories lie.

In faded photos, their faces gleam,
Fragments of moments, lost in a dream.
They hide in the silence, yet fill the space,
With whispers of love, time can't erase.

Footsteps retrace where children would play,
Ghosts in the laughter, brightening the gray.
Each chuckle a heartbeat, a tale to unfold,
Stories of warmth in the shadows retold.

Yet silence envelopes the corners so dear,
Memories dance in the atmosphere.
Lost are the echoes of joyous nights,
In shadows of laughter, their spirit ignites.

Oh, how they linger, those breaths of the past,
Silhouettes fading, yet meant to last.
In every whisper, in every glance,
Forgotten laughter in a timeless dance.

Fragments of What Was

Scattered pieces of long-lost days,
In every corner, a memory plays.
Traces of smiles that vanished too fast,
In the silence, whispers of the past.

A worn-out book with pages torn,
Stories of love, of hearts once worn.
In dusty corners, they cling to the light,
Fragments of lives that felt so right.

Each photograph a portal wide,
To laughter shared, to joy and pride.
Yet time's cruel hand has left its mark,
In the distance, echoes grow stark.

The breeze carries soft, aching sighs,
Of moments that linger beneath the skies.
Each breath a reminder, each thought a wound,
In the cracks of our souls, they are marooned.

Still, hope flickers in the lingering glow,
Fragments of what was, refuse to go.
A tapestry woven in heartstrings weak,
In every silence, they quietly speak.

Embraced by Absence

In the void where laughter used to lie,
Shadows gather, though no one is nigh.
Embraced by absence, a lingering ache,
The heart feels heavy, each breath a quake.

Whispers of memories softly creep,
In the corners where silence sleeps.
Remnants of joy, like leaves in a storm,
A bittersweet echo, a fading warm.

Moments once shared, like autumn leaves,
Drifting away, yet the heart believes.
In the stillness, their essence remains,
A melody sweet, laced with pain.

The clock ticks on, unyielding, bold,
Yet time can't sever the bonds, we hold.
In every heartbeat, their spirits thrive,
Embraced by absence, we still survive.

Through the shadows, we seek the light,
Finding solace in the depth of night.
For in absence, love's echoes linger near,
Stitching together the fabric of fear.

The Forgotten Serenade

In shadows cast by evening light,
A melody lost, an echo slight.
Whispers dance upon the breeze,
Hiding secrets among the trees.

With every note, a memory fades,
In tranquil woods where silence wades.
The heartstring plucks, a gentle sigh,
A song of love that dares not die.

Yet time forgets what once was sweet,
As dreams dissolve beneath our feet.
The serenade calls, yet none can hear,
A haunting tune, both far and near.

Hope lingers in the dusk's embrace,
A forgotten tune, a fleeting trace.
In twilight moments, we reminisce,
Of tender times that we might miss.

But every note holds what we seek,
A melody strong, though it feels weak.
In each soft chord, a life to live,
The serenade whispers what hearts forgive.

The Sweetness of Fleeting Time

Like morning dew on soft green leaves,
Time slips away as the heart believes.
Each passing hour, a gentle sigh,
A moment captured, a sweet goodbye.

With laughter bright, we chase the sun,
In every heartbeat, we're all but one.
The clock ticks softly, a tender chime,
Reminding us of the sweetness of time.

Yet shadows grow as daylight wanes,
In every joy, a hint of pains.
We dance through life, our spirits high,
But every laugh must learn to cry.

Through whispered dreams and quiet nights,
We savor love's soft, fleeting lights.
In moments shared, we find our rhyme,
A harmony woven in the fabric of time.

So let us cherish each passing glance,
In the tapestry of life, we dance.
The sweetness lingers in every heart,
As fleeting moments become our art.

Unwritten Chapters

The pages blank, a story waits,
With ink still fresh upon the slates.
Each heart a tale, each dream a line,
In unwritten chapters, destinies twine.

With every choice, a twist unfolds,
A path unraveled, a truth that holds.
Through whispered hopes and silent fears,
We pen our lives with love and tears.

The quill in hand, the thoughts take flight,
In darkest hours or brightest light.
The journey beckons, wild and free,
To find the words that speak of me.

As moments gather like falling leaves,
The unwritten chapters weave beliefs.
In tapestries of laughter and grace,
Each story shared finds its place.

So let us write without regret,
In every verse, our souls be met.
The unwritten future waits to be,
A tale of life, of you and me.

Whispers in the Twilight

Softly the night begins to fall,
Gentle shadows stretch and crawl.
Leaves rustle with secrets to share,
In the hush, we linger, aware.

Stars twinkle in the dusky skies,
As daylight finally bids goodbye.
Echoes dance on the cool evening air,
In this moment, we find our care.

Moonlight spills through the trees,
Carrying a calm, soothing breeze.
Whispers of dreams call us near,
As darkness wraps us without fear.

Footsteps quiet on the path ahead,
Tracing where our hearts have led.
Each glance holds a tale untold,
In the twilight, our souls unfold.

Together we savor the night's embrace,
In the silence, we find our place.
Whispers weaving a soft refrain,
In the twilight, love will remain.

Hidden Glances

In crowded rooms, our eyes collide,
Silent promises we try to hide.
The world around fades to gray,
While hidden glances lead the way.

Moments captured in fleeting sighs,
Tension builds beneath our lies.
Unspoken words linger in the air,
Brushing past with an electric flair.

As laughter bubbles, our hearts race,
In secret corners, we find our space.
A gentle touch, our fingers trace,
In hidden glances, we find our grace.

Time stands still, the noise subsides,
In your eyes, a thousand tides.
With every blink, a story shared,
In the depths, we know we dared.

The evening wanes, but still we stay,
Lost in this dance, we hesitate.
Though words may falter, love knows chance,
In our hearts, hidden glances prance.

The Tapestry of Brief Encounters

Threads of moments intertwine,
Each encounter a spark divine.
Faces fade, but spirits remain,
In the tapestry, woven with pain.

A stranger's smile, a fleeting touch,
Fragments of life that mean so much.
Together we laugh, then drift apart,
In this weave, you touch my heart.

Chapters written in borrowed time,
Shared stories dance in rhythm and rhyme.
Every glance, a stitch we create,
In the rich fabric, woven by fate.

In the tapestry, colors blend,
Friendships form, and some may end.
Yet each thread holds a story true,
A reminder of moments shared with you.

As time moves on, we hold what's real,
In the tapestry, we learn to heal.
Though brief, these meetings leave a trace,
A woven memory, a sacred space.

Dancing with Shadows

Beneath the moon's soft, silver glow,
We twirl with shadows, stealing the show.
Flickering lights lead the way,
In the night, we choose to sway.

Whispers flutter on the breeze,
As we dance among the trees.
Footprints fade in silvery dust,
In this moment, we learn to trust.

Shadows stretch and curve with grace,
Embracing every hidden space.
Through laughter, we chase away the fears,
In the dance, we shed our tears.

With every step, the world falls away,
In the darkness, we find our play.
Together we move, free from shame,
In this rhythm, we're all the same.

As dawn beckons with gentle light,
The shadows whisper their soft goodnight.
But in our hearts, the dance will remain,
To remind us of joy, and moments gained.

When Minutes Collide

Time slows down, a gentle sigh,
Moments blend, as days slip by.
Ticking clocks begin to fade,
Life's sweet symphony, softly played.

In the rush, a glance is shared,
Silent whispers, feelings bared.
Eternal seconds, hearts entwined,
In this dance, what love can find.

Memories whirl like autumn leaves,
In the chaos, the heart believes.
Fragmented time, yet whole we feel,
As minutes crash, our fates conceal.

In twilight's glow, we find our place,
Every heartbeat, an embrace.
Two souls shimmer in starlit skies,
Lost in the moment, where magic lies.

Disguised Glances

Eyes that meet, yet hearts conceal,
A fleeting spark, an unspoken deal.
In crowded rooms, we play our parts,
Veiled intentions, guarded hearts.

Silent words, like shadows cast,
Each look exchanged, a story vast.
Secrets linger, as we pretend,
A dance of fate, where longing bends.

In the night, we steal our chance,
Wrapped in silence, a hidden dance.
Cloaked in mystery, feelings grow,
As undiscovered paths bestow.

Amidst the noise, we find our space,
In the clamor, a woven grace.
With every glance, the tension tight,
In the shadows, love ignites.

Abandoned Lullabies

Softly sung in twilight's breath,
Melodies linger, whispering death.
Forgotten dreams, in silence rest,
Lost in echoes, a heart's unrest.

Faded tunes of yesteryear,
Strains of joy turned into fear.
Once embraced in tender light,
Now just shadows of the night.

Cradled gently by the breeze,
Haunting waves, as time decrees.
Each note a tale of love once bright,
Now a ghost in the pale moonlight.

Yet we cling to what remains,
In the quiet, a soft refrain.
For in the dark, hope still sings,
Amidst the sorrow, a new heart clings.

The Intersection of Dreams

Where visions cross, our hopes collide,
In the twilight, we must decide.
Paths entwined with whispered fate,
Infinite realms, we navigate.

In the silence, truths emerge,
Fear and courage begin to surge.
Every choice a twist of time,
In shared stillness, we learn to climb.

Painted skies, our futures flare,
In every heartbeat, dreams laid bare.
With open hearts, we choose to soar,
On wings of visions, we explore.

In this moment, worlds unite,
Through the shadows, we find the light.
At the crossroads of belief,
Love guides us forth, beyond relief.

Threads of the Forgotten

In shadows deep where secrets lie,
Memories weave like dreams in the sky.
Faded tales of laughter and woe,
Lost in the echoes of long ago.

Beneath the stars, whispers float,
Carried on winds that gently emote.
Each thread a story, a life once spun,
In the quiet corners, their dance is done.

The tapestry holds both joy and pain,
A fragile beauty that still can remain.
With every knot, a heartbeat sings,
In the silence, the past still clings.

Though time may fade the vibrant hue,
The golden strands still shine bright and true.
In the tapestry of what we've taught,
Lie the threads of the forgotten, now caught.

So gather close, hear the old refrain,
Of moments lost, but never in vain.
For in the fabric of night and day,
The threads of our stories forever will stay.

A Dance Half Remembered

In twilight's grace, a whisper flows,
A dance half remembered, as time slows.
Footsteps trace where shadows loom,
Echoing laughter in the dusk's gloom.

Under the moon's soft silver gaze,
The night unveils its nostalgic haze.
With every twirl, the heart takes flight,
In the stillness of the gentle night.

Unseen partners glide through the air,
In every heartbeat, a secret prayer.
Lost melodies softly resound,
In the silence, the souls are found.

Each turn a memory, each leap a sigh,
In the dance of yesteryears gone by.
The world fades, leaving only the beat,
As dreams and reality gracefully meet.

But with the dawn, the music fades,
Yet the dance lives on in the glades.
For though we part, the rhythm stays,
In shadows and light, it forever plays.

Whispers of the Past

In quiet corners where memories dwell,
Whispers of the past weave their spell.
Faint echoes call from days gone by,
A gentle reminder of how time sighs.

Pages turn with a soft rustle,
A story lingers, never to bustle.
Each voice a flicker, each glance a spark,
Illuminating paths once lost in the dark.

Through crumbling pages and fading light,
The tales emerge, taking to flight.
In soft whispers, the past unfolds,
Breathing life into forgotten golds.

With every story, a lesson learned,
In the warmth of the heart, memories burned.
Though years may pass and shadows fall,
The whispers of the past call to us all.

So listen closely to the gentle breeze,
In its soft cadence, the heart finds ease.
For in the echoes where we once laughed,
Lie the whispers of the past, a cherished craft.

The Lullaby of Time

In the hush of twilight, time softly sighs,
A lullaby woven beneath starlit skies.
Cradling moments, both fleeting and dear,
In the arms of the night, our dreams reappear.

The moon spins tales with her silvery thread,
While shadows dance gently, in silence they tread.
Each heartbeat a note in the symphony grand,
In the lullaby of time, together we stand.

As seasons shift, and the years drift away,
The song of the present holds memories at bay.
In the cadence of life, rich stories entwine,
Carried by breezes, through clocks that align.

So let us embrace what the evening bestows,
In whispers of time, where love gently grows.
For every moment is a precious rhyme,
Humming forever in the lullaby of time.

In twilight's embrace, as the shadows may fall,
The gift of tomorrow beckons us all.
For in each fleeting heartbeat, a promise shines,
In the cradle of moments, the lullaby binds.

The Hourglass Dancer

In shadows cast by waning light,
A dancer sways with pure delight.
Her feet caress the drifting sands,
Each grain a tale in delicate hands.

The hourglass spills its fleeting time,
With every move, she starts to climb.
The music plays, a sweet embrace,
As moments fade, she finds her place.

She twirls within the ticking sound,
A rhythm lost, yet always found.
In every step, a breath of grace,
She dances on, defies the space.

With whispers soft, the night unfolds,
Her story whispered, yet untold.
In twilight's glow, her spirit glides,
The hourglass holds what time divides.

A final bow beneath the moon,
The dancer fades, yet leaves a tune.
For in her heart, the sands remain,
In every pulse, the dance sustains.

Secrets at Twilight

When twilight wraps the world in glow,
The whispered secrets start to flow.
In every hush, a tale resides,
Where dreams and shadows dare to hide.

Beneath the stars, the night reveals,
The softest touch of hope it steals.
A silver moon climbs high above,
With every beam, it sings of love.

The trees embrace with ancient sighs,
As fireflies dance in evening skies.
A breeze carries a muffled laugh,
In twilight's arms, we find our path.

Each heartbeat echoes, soft and clear,
Awakening the hidden sphere.
In whispered tones, the world unfolds,
As twilight's tapestry is told.

So gather close, let secrets flow,
In twilight's grasp, we come to know.
That every dusk will softly hint,
Of mysteries in which we're mint.

Memories Like Fireflies

In summer's dusk, the fireflies gleam,
They dance upon the whispered dream.
Each flicker holds a time long past,
A moment captured, fleeting, fast.

They float like thoughts on gentle streams,
Reminding us of softer themes.
With every flicker, stories bloom,
Memories spark by glowing gloom.

A child's laughter, a lover's gaze,
In tiny lights, the heart obeys.
They guide us through the shadowed night,
Leading us toward a purest light.

The dance of time, forever spins,
In fragile glow, the journey begins.
Each firefly carries what we seek,
The brightest joys, the tender peaks.

As darkness folds the world in grace,
We find ourselves in firefly space.
In every glow, a part of us,
Memories linger, bright and thus.

Fragments of a Forgotten Smile

In dusty corners of the mind,
A smile rests, no longer kind.
It sparkles faintly in the light,
A ghost of joy that fades from sight.

Once it danced on lips so wide,
A bridge of warmth, a joyful tide.
But time has swept its face away,
Leaving only shadows of the day.

A photograph in colors pale,
Of laughter lost, a wistful tale.
It lingers like a fading song,
A fragment where we once belonged.

Yet in the quiet, hope remains,
To piece together joy from pain.
For fragments tell of what was true,
And in the shards, we find the new.

So cherish each brief, shining sight,
For smiles can bloom in darkest night.
With gentle hands, we'll stitch and style,
Reviving lost, forgotten smile.

The Thief's Silent Waltz

In shadows deep, he twirls with grace,
A silent thief, in twilight's embrace.
Footsteps whisper, secrets unfold,
In the night, his stories are told.

Moonlight flickers on stolen dreams,
Where silence lingers and softly beams.
Each stolen glance, a dance of fate,
In the stillness, they hesitate.

A heart that beats in measured time,
He weaves through hours, a silent rhyme.
Echoes of laughter through the dark,
His presence leaves a haunting mark.

A phantom's waltz, enticing and real,
In every step, a fated deal.
A hug of shadows, a sweet embrace,
The thief in night's most secret place.

As dawn approaches, he slips away,
Leaving whispers at the break of day.
The silent waltz, a fading art,
In every theft, he steals a heart.

Breaths between Heartbeats

In the quiet between, life unfolds,
Moments linger, gently enfold.
Whispers of time, soft and slow,
Each breath dances, a silent flow.

In the pause, stories find their grace,
As silence wraps a warm embrace.
Waiting souls in twilight pause,
Seeking answers, without cause.

A heartbeat thrums in the still,
Echoes of hope, the soul to fill.
Between each pulse, the dreams ignite,
Carries the weight of futile fight.

Lingering thoughts, like shadows glide,
Through the stillness, they abide.
Life's rhythm, a delicate thread,
In breaths exchanged, the unsaid.

With every sigh, the heart will weave,
A tapestry of love and leave.
In quiet breaths, lives intertwine,
In heartbeats' dance, we are divine.

Fleeting Aspects of You

In the breeze, your laughter plays,
A moment's glance, a sunlit haze.
Shadows cast by your fleeting light,
Glimmers, whispers, taking flight.

Every smile, a fleeting spark,
Fading like the evening's dark.
Captured in time, then swiftly gone,
Fleeting aspects linger on.

Your voice, a melody, soft and sweet,
In echoes, where our lives repeat.
Even silence sings your tune,
In shadows cast by the silver moon.

Moments stolen, breaths of air,
Each memory a precious dare.
Time races on, relentless and true,
Grasping fleeting aspects of you.

In fleeting dreams, you often roam,
A spirit searching for a home.
In the spaces where we connect,
Fleeting aspects, hearts respect.

Interval of a Dream

In the hush before the night unveils,
Whispers float on gentle gales.
A moment paused, a sigh held tight,
In the interval, dreams take flight.

Stars begin their soft ballet,
A dance of light, guiding the way.
Thoughts meander through velvet skies,
Trapped in the night, where hope defies.

Shadows shift, the world feels near,
In this stillness, we conquer fear.
Between eye blinks, futures unfold,
In intervals, the dreams are bold.

A heartbeat echoes in the dark,
Guiding whispers, a yearning spark.
In the hush of night, we find our way,
Through intervals where colors play.

As dawn approaches, dreams take flight,
In each promise, a guiding light.
In the interval, our hearts align,
In dreams, forever, we entwine.

A Moment's Breath

In the hush of dawn's first light,
A whisper drifts, softly bright.
Time pauses gently, a fragile thread,
Holding dreams, where silence is spread.

Nature breathes in a calm embrace,
Moments linger, leaving no trace.
The world awakens with a sigh,
As night's shadows begin to fly.

Crisp air dances upon pale skin,
Filled with the warmth that stirs within.
Each heartbeat echoes in the still,
Drawing life from the morning's will.

A fleeting pause, a glance, a smile,
We stand together, just for a while.
In the simplicity of this grace,
We find our place, a sacred space.

So breathe in deep, let worries cease,
In this moment, feel the peace.
For time stands still, just for today,
As dreams unfold and drift away.

Where Shadows Rest

Beneath the boughs, in twilight's glow,
Whispers of time begin to flow.
Shadows gather, soft and slow,
In corners where forgotten dreams go.

Silent stories the night reveals,
As darkness wraps in its gentle seals.
Echoes of laughter, distant calls,
In the hush, where silence falls.

Memories linger, like old friends,
Tracing paths where the journey bends.
In muted tones, the past speaks clear,
In every shadow that draws near.

The moonlight casts a silver thread,
Where hopes and fears often tread.
We walk the line, both lost and found,
In this realm where dreams abound.

And as we pause to catch our breath,
In this sanctuary, where shadows rest.
We find the light amidst the dark,
A flicker, a flame, a tiny spark.

Charms of a Distant Past

Old photographs in frames of gold,
Treasured tales of times retold.
Each smile a memory, each gaze a glance,
Unlocking echoes of a fleeting dance.

Laughter weaves through the faded years,
Dancing lightly, soothing fears.
Moments etched in the heart's embrace,
The sweetest charms, a gentle grace.

Starlit nights and lazy days,
Whispers of love in countless ways.
Time may fade, but feelings stay,
In the realm of yesterday.

Familiar faces, the warmth of home,
Through meadows wild, we freely roam.
A tapestry of lives entwined,
In the charms of what we find.

Each cherished thought, a timeless link,
In the pulse of life, we gently sink.
For in the past, we find our way,
Guiding us to each new day.

Reflections on the Water's Edge

Crystal ripples on a silver lake,
Mirrored skies for the heart to take.
Each glance a glimpse into the soul,
Where silent depths make us whole.

Rippling whispers on the breeze,
Swirling thoughts like dancing leaves.
Time flows gently, a steady stream,
In these waters, we dare to dream.

With each wave, a story unfolds,
Of love, of loss, of secrets told.
The surface shimmers, hiding the past,
In depths where memories are cast.

We kneel down, touch the edge with care,
As reflections swirl in the evening air.
The dance of shadows and light's caress,
In this moment, we find our rest.

So linger here, where waters flow,
Embrace the stillness, let go.
For on this edge, we come alive,
In reflections deep, our spirits thrive.

Light Trapped in Glass

Sunlight dances on the pane,
Fleeting shadows, bright refrain.
Moments caught, no escape,
In the frame, dreams shape.

Whispers of the world outside,
Timeless secrets trapped inside.
Reflecting hopes, a spectrum's play,
In stillness, they softly sway.

A prism's glow, a gentle touch,
Yet within, it feels so much.
Fractured beams, a tender hue,
Glass confines what we pursue.

Imagined worlds beyond the glass,
Where wishes stir, and spirits pass.
Yet here we linger, caught in light,
Searching for the stars at night.

In silence, tales remain untold,
The joys and sorrows, bright and bold.
Frozen moments whisper low,
In crystal confines, love can grow.

The Heart's Hidden Memoir

In pages worn, the stories hum,
Each heartbeat echoes, a distant drum.
Ink bleeds dreams in shades of grace,
Chronicles penned, our secret place.

Emotions spill, like rain from skies,
Beneath the words, the truth lies.
Whispers linger, soft and clear,
Stories echo, year to year.

A tender hand, a fleeting smile,
Captured moments, worth the while.
Hidden desires tattooed in prose,
In every chapter, the heart's repose.

The ink may fade, yet feelings stay,
Timeless echoes will not stray.
With every line, a tear, a laugh,
The heart's memoir, our precious path.

So write your truths, don't hold them back,
Bring forth the love from shadows black.
In parchment bound, our souls entwined,
In memoirs deep, our hearts aligned.

Celestial Echoes

Stars shimmer like forgotten dreams,
Whispers float on cosmic beams.
Galaxies spin in graceful flight,
Wonders weave through velvet night.

In silence vast, the void unfolds,
Stories untold, the cosmos holds.
Light-years pass, time stands still,
Echoes linger, a cosmic thrill.

Planets dance in harmonious way,
A celestial tune, night and day.
Comets blaze, they rise and fall,
In their wake, they beckon all.

Nebulae bloom in colors rare,
In the darkness, beauty fair.
Constellations chart our fate,
Guiding hearts across the great.

So gaze above, let wonder soar,
In the stars, we're evermore.
Each twinkle holds a secret true,
A celestial echo, just for you.

Landscapes of What Once Was

Empty streets where laughter thrived,
In faded dreams, the past survived.
Whispers of joy, now silent sighs,
In memories held, our heart replies.

Cracked pavements tell of days gone by,
Where sunlight painted the endless sky.
Each shadow cast holds a story deep,
In lost landscapes, our spirits weep.

Houses stand with windows bare,
Rusting gates, a lingering stare.
Forgotten gardens bloom in dust,
Nature's reclaim, a tender trust.

Yet in the silence, beauty grows,
In every wound, a petal shows.
Through time's passage, hope won't cease,
From ashes rise a spark of peace.

So wander through what once was known,
In every crack, seeds are sown.
Landscapes speak of love and loss,
In shattered dreams, we'll find our gloss.

Unraveled Threads of Yesterday

In shadows cast by fading light,
I trace the paths of dreams once bright.
Each moment whispers, soft and low,
The tales of where my heart would go.

Through tangled knots, the memories weave,
Of laughter shared, and moments cleaved.
Yet time unspools the golden thread,
Leaving echoes of words unsaid.

With every stitch, a story told,
Of fragile love, and hearts of gold.
Yet in the seams, a fracture lies,
As yesterday's embrace slowly dies.

The fabric worn, the colors fade,
What once was bright now starts to jade.
I gather remnants of my past,
Each thread a memory that won't last.

But in the silence, I still find,
The beauty in the ties that bind.
Though unraveling, the fibers stay,
A tapestry of yesterday.

Pockets of Eternity

In fleeting seconds, treasures hide,
Moments captured, a timeless ride.
Soft whispers in a gentle breeze,
Pockets of love, memories that tease.

Each heartbeat echoes, loud and true,
A symphony of me and you.
Laughter dances on the air,
In every glance, we find our share.

The ticking clock may steal our time,
Yet in these pockets, love will climb.
With every touch, eternity glows,
In tiny fragments, our essence flows.

Through sunlit days and starry nights,
We stitch together, wrongs and rights.
In every pulse, we hold the key,
To pockets filled with harmony.

So let the world rush by, unkind,
For in this space, our hearts aligned.
In moments small, we find our worth,
In pockets of eternity's mirth.

Time's Elusive Caress

In whispers soft, time glides away,
A delicate dance of night and day.
Like grains of sand through fingers slip,
Moments cherished on a fleeting trip.

The clock's embrace a measured beat,
Yet in its grasp, love feels so sweet.
Through every hour, a tender grace,
In time's elusive, warm embrace.

We chase the dawn, we chase the dusk,
In every breath, a quiet trust.
For though it fades, we hold it close,
In tiny sparks, the warmth we chose.

So let the shadows kiss the light,
And wrap us in their soft delight.
For even as the hours wane,
Time's caress, our love will gain.

In moments fleeting, we will find,
The beauty in what's left behind.
For time's embrace, though quick and stern,
Bears the lessons we will learn.

Memories Wrapped in Silence

In quiet corners of my mind,
Memories linger, softly blind.
Wrapped in silence, echoes grow,
Tales of love that only we know.

Each heartbeat carries stories old,
Of whispered dreams and truths we hold.
Through silence thick, our laughter flows,
In shadows deep, affection grows.

The stillness wraps us, warm and tight,
As day dissolves into the night.
In every pause, a world unfolds,
In silence, deep, our heart consoled.

Though words may falter, feelings remain,
In tender glances, joy and pain.
For wrapped in silence, we find the way,
Our memories dance, come what may.

So let the world around us fade,
In silence, love's serenade.
For memories wrapped in quiet grace,
Are treasures time cannot erase.

A Symphony of Fleeting Moments

Notes drift softly on the breeze,
Echoes of laughter blend with trees.
A gentle whisper, a fleeting glance,
Time unravels in a dance.

Stars awaken in the night,
Illuminating hearts so bright.
Each heartbeat's a fleeting sound,
In this symphony, love is found.

Moments slip like grains of sand,
Drawn by fate's delicate hand.
We cherish each blink of an eye,
As the world rushes swiftly by.

Waves crash softly on the shore,
Memories linger, begging for more.
In the silence, we find our song,
In fleeting moments, we belong.

So let us savor every beat,
The rush of life, bitter yet sweet.
In this symphony, together we rise,
A chorus beneath the endless skies.

The Brief Affair of Time

Time is a lover, fleeting and sweet,
A tender kiss that we can't repeat.
It brushes our skin like a soft breeze,
Leaving us longing, begging for ease.

Days turn to whispers, nights into sighs,
Moments are treasures, disguised in goodbyes.
A glance, a touch, and then it's gone,
The brief affair beckons at dawn.

Ticking clocks mark the dance of fate,
As seconds merge into one fleeting state.
We chase shadows, we dream and we run,
Yet time's quick embrace leaves us undone.

In the silence where memories bloom,
We gather lost dreams from the gloom.
Though time may slip through our hands like sand,
In our hearts its echoes will always stand.

So hold on tight to each fleeting kiss,
In the brief affair, we find our bliss.
Though time is transient, cruelly unknown,
In each stolen moment, we are never alone.

Moments in a Bottle

Captured whispers, a treasure to keep,
Moments in a bottle, memories deep.
A laugh, a tear, a gentle embrace,
Time frozen in glass, a sacred space.

The tides of life ebb and flow,
Each drop a story, a seed to sow.
Through the years, the bottles align,
Holding the echoes of hearts entwined.

Sunsets trapped in crystal light,
Starlit dances that grace the night.
Every sip brings waves of delight,
Drunken on dreams, we take to flight.

Sealed with hope, each moment stays,
A journey of love in countless ways.
When the world feels heavy, just uncork,
And let the magic of memories spark.

So raise your bottle, toast to the past,
Embrace the fleeting, hold it fast.
For life's a collection, a beautiful scroll,
Moments in a bottle that nourish the soul.

The Light Between Us

In shadows cast by fleeting days,
A spark ignites in whispered rays.
The light between us softly glows,
Bridging the gap where love flows.

Stars collide in the darkest night,
Guiding our hearts toward the light.
With every glance, electric and bright,
We paint the silence, chasing the night.

Through time's tangled web we weave,
In the warmth of love, we believe.
Moments shared, so precious, so few,
In the light between us, dreams feel true.

As twilight whispers, the world takes pause,
In quiet corners, there's no more cause.
Only the light that dances and plays,
Illuminating our countless days.

So let us linger, hand in hand,
In the glow of moments, forever we'll stand.
For the light between us, strong and divine,
Is the tether of hearts, eternally intertwined.

The Invisibility of Now

Moments slip through fingers fine,
In the rush of heartbeats chime.
We chase the shadows of the past,
Yet here we stand, the die is cast.

Whispers of the present fade,
As dreams in daylight quickly wade.
Time's embrace, a fleeting friend,
Each second lost, no chance to mend.

Glimmers of joy, they come and go,
Like autumn leaves, a soft tableau.
We long for stillness, crave the now,
But time's quick hand won't bend or bow.

In every breath, a choice to make,
In every heartbeat, sweet stakes awake.
The present calls, yet we ignore,
As we search for forevermore.

The invisibility of this moment,
Is the truth that we often torment.
To live each day, to feel it flow,
Is the art of savoring the glow.

Twilights of What Could Be

Under purple skies we dream,
Hopes adrift on a silver stream.
In the twilight, visions gleam,
Whispers linger, soft and extreme.

Paths not taken, shadows cast,
Faded futures, fleeting fast.
What could be haunts every sigh,
In silence echoes, 'why oh why?'

With every star that begins to rise,
A canvas painted in our eyes.
Limitless worlds that beckon near,
Yet in our hands, we hold the fear.

Twilight stretches, holds its breath,
A promise lingers, not just death.
In dreams, we wander, hopes ignite,
What could be blurs into the night.

So let us seek these fleeting lands,
With open hearts and willing hands.
The twilight's glow, a chance to see,
The boundless realms of what could be.

Short-lived Serenades

A melody drifts on evening air,
Notes like raindrops, light and rare.
In this moment, heartbeats rhyme,
But fleeting songs can't pause for time.

Sweet whispers linger, moments shared,
Yet like petals, they have been bared.
Every note a puff of smoke,
In the night, the silence broke.

Short-lived serenades, soft and fleet,
Leave impressions where memories meet.
In the twilight, echoes fade,
Lost in shadows, music played.

We chase the echoes, hold them tight,
But they slip away into the night.
As we dance to a tune so sweet,
We learn that endings can't be beat.

Cherish the sounds, though brief they be,
In their whispers, we find the key.
For every song that comes and goes,
Leaves a trace, like soft rose blows.

The Secret Garden of Lost Time

Behind the walls of thoughts confined,
A garden blooms, where few can find.
In shadows deep, lost dreams reside,
Whispers of echoes, time's sweet tide.

Each flower holds a memory dear,
Of laughter, tears, and silent fear.
Captured moments, forever young,
In every petal, sweetly sung.

A hidden path where moments stray,
The echoes of our yesterday.
We wander through the blooms of age,
Each step a turn, a timeless page.

Lost time whispers in gentle tones,
Reminds us of our joys and moans.
In the secret garden's embrace,
We find ourselves in a sacred space.

So let us tend this garden wild,
With care and love, like a child.
For in this realm of what we seek,
The secret garden speaks, unique.

Embraced by Twilight

The sun bows low, the sky aglow,
Stars awaken, a gentle show.
Whispers of night in the cooling air,
Nature's secrets, everywhere.

Shadows linger, dance and sway,
Fleeting moments at the end of day.
Moonlight drapes the world in peace,
In twilight's arms, all worries cease.

Crickets sing in soft refrain,
A melody that soothes the pain.
Dreams take flight on silken wings,
As night unfolds, the heart it brings.

In the hush, the night unfolds,
A tapestry of secrets told.
Through every breath, the beauty grows,
In twilight's grasp, the spirit glows.

Unraveled Dreams

In the quiet of night, visions appear,
Threads once woven now frayed with fear.
A tapestry bright, now torn at the seams,
Lost in the realm of unravelled dreams.

Colors collide in a chaotic dance,
Fleeting moments, a fragile chance.
Hope hangs precarious, like dew on the grass,
Every heartbeat, a whisper to pass.

Fragments of joy, shadows of doubt,
Echoes of laughter, we ponder about.
Through whispers of longing, we search for the light,
In the depth of the darkness, we try to ignite.

But woven within the faintest of threads,
Are the memories cherished, the paths that we tread.
So hold onto dreams, though they seem lost,
For every unraveling comes with a cost.

Hushed Reveries

In still moments, silence sings,
The heart finds peace in simple things.
Gentle breezes caress the soul,
As whispered secrets make us whole.

Stars intimate with the sleeping night,
Casting dreams in ethereal light.
As shadows dance, we drift away,
To realms of wonder where hearts can play.

Each breath a story, softly told,
In hushed reveries, the world unfolds.
Through muffled echoes of time gone past,
We find our solace, our shadows cast.

In the quiet, new hopes arise,
As night enchants with moonlit skies.
In every thought, a magical flight,
In whispered wishes, we hold on tight.

Time Slips Through Fingers

Grains of sand in the hourglass fall,
Moments fleeting, we heed their call.
With every tick, the clock unwinds,
And echoes of laughter are left behind.

Days turn to whispers, flowing fast,
We cling to memories, shadows cast.
Each second sacred, yet swift as a stream,
A dance of existence, a delicate dream.

In the rush of life, we often forget,
To savor the present, no room for regret.
With open hearts and clear, bright eyes,
We gather the moments, let spirits rise.

Time, like water, slips through our hands,
But love remains, like uncharted lands.
So cherish the now, let your heart sing,
In each fleeting moment, find the spring.

Echoes in the Silence

In whispered tones of twilight's grace,
Shadows dance in a quiet space.
The heartbeats fade, the stars ignite,
In the stillness, dreams take flight.

Memories linger, soft and clear,
Crafting stories we hold dear.
Among the hush, a voice will rise,
In echoes, love never dies.

The moonlight bathes the world in gold,
Tales of old through silence told.
Each sigh a note, each glance a song,
In this quiet, we belong.

Time stands still in the night's embrace,
Lost in moments we cannot trace.
Yet in the silence, there's a spark,
Guiding us through the endless dark.

As dawn approaches, light unfurls,
Revealing secrets of hidden worlds.
In echoes soft, our spirits blend,
In silence, we are never alone, my friend.

The Artwork of Absence

In spaces left by what is lost,
We find a beauty, at what cost?
Silent canvases paint the air,
With strokes of time, a tender care.

Faded signs of laughter's trace,
In every corner, a soft embrace.
The heart remembers, though still it sighs,
In absence, love never truly dies.

We gather fragments, piece by piece,
In the quiet, longing finds release.
With every breath, a tale unfolds,
Of whispered thoughts and dreams of old.

What remains is a gentle light,
Guiding shadows into the night.
With every heartbeat, we recreate,
This artwork shaped by love and fate.

Absence breathes in colors bold,
Whispered stories still to be told.
In the void, we learn to see,
The silent echoes setting us free.

Remnants of a Gentle Kiss

On lips that linger, night takes hold,
A memory soft, a story told.
With whispers sweet as the twilight breeze,
We find our peace among the trees.

Each touch ignites a spark divine,
In stolen moments, hearts entwine.
The echo of love, so pure, so bright,
In remnants found in the cool of night.

Time may fade, yet we remain,
Bound by laughter, love, and pain.
In every sigh, a promise missed,
The haunting trace of a gentle kiss.

And when the dawn breaks through the dark,
Our hearts still hold that precious spark.
As memories dance, they softly gleam,
In shadows spun from love's own dream.

Though moments pass and seasons change,
The remnants linger, sweet and strange.
In every heartbeat, a world exists,
A tapestry of love's own twists.

Captured by the Wind

A soft caress through rustling leaves,
Whispers tell of what one believes.
The world spins round, yet we stand still,
Bound by dreams and the heart's own will.

The wind carries whispers of the past,
Each fleeting moment meant to last.
With every breeze, a memory stirs,
In the air, our laughter purrs.

Clouds drift by on the canvas sky,
While wishes take their flight and fly.
Captured in currents, our souls ascend,
In the embrace of the wind's sweet blend.

In fields of gold where wildflowers sway,
Nature sings in its vibrant display.
We dance together, hearts aligned,
In the freedom space, time unwinds.

As the twilight fades into night's embrace,
The wind carries home our softest grace.
Every sigh, a love letter penned,
A journey begun, with no end.

Chronicles of the Unseen

In shadows deep, where whispers dwell,
The tales of yore, they softly tell.
Of ancient trees with branches wide,
And secrets kept, where dreams reside.

A flicker here, a glance for sure,
The unseen paths that we endure.
Through woven fates and silent cries,
In hidden realms, the truth belies.

With every breath, a story fades,
In echoes soft, where memory wades.
The silence speaks of lost embraces,
And unfound love in distant places.

Yet in the gloom, a spark ignites,
Illuminating quiet nights.
With every turn, new light is cast,
In chronicles of shadows past.

Kaleidoscope of Memory

Fragments of color swirl and blend,
Each hue a tale, each twist a bend.
Times we laughed, and moments shared,
A tapestry of feelings dared.

Reflections dance in playful light,
Memories twinkle, shining bright.
Through fragile glass, the past takes form,
In every storm, a heart keeps warm.

The echoes fade, but never die,
In whispered songs, we dare to fly.
Each shifting scene, a treasure found,
In kaleidoscope, love's truth abound.

So twist the lens, let colors show,
The beauty in what we used to know.
In every shard, a piece of time,
The dance of life, a perfect rhyme.

Fleeting Glances

In crowded rooms, our eyes do meet,
A moment's spark, so bittersweet.
A fleeting glance, a silent call,
Yet time stands still, we risk it all.

The world around fades into gray,
In shared breath, we drift away.
With every heartbeat, secrets bloom,
In gentle smiles, dispel the gloom.

But time it moves, a ruthless thief,
Stealing moments, bringing grief.
Yet every glance, a world unfolds,
A story of hearts, forever told.

So cherish well that brief exchange,
In the dance of life, so strange.
For in the briefest look, we see,
The depth of love, the mystery.

The Diary of What Was

Pages worn with time's embrace,
Ink of memories, we retrace.
In every line, a heartbeat's sound,
A diary where our truths are found.

The laughter echoes, soft and pure,
In handwritten dreams that still allure.
With every tear, the pages sigh,
The ink can't fade, it dares to fly.

A glimpse of faces, lines of fate,
In crumpled sheets, we contemplate.
What was once bright, now softly glows,
In silent whispers, love still flows.

So turn the pages, let them speak,
In every word, the heart is weak.
The diary of what has been,
A tapestry of where we've seen.

Savoring the Elusive

The morning dew glistens bright,
Each droplet holds a dream in sight.
Whispers of time, sweetly unfold,
As memories dance, both young and old.

A fleeting glance, a moment rare,
We chase the light in the morning air.
With each heartbeat, we seize the day,
Savoring life in a tender way.

Colors blend in a gentle hue,
Painting stories, both old and new.
In silence shared, secrets are found,
Echoing softly, love unbound.

Almonds and roses, scents intertwine,
In gardens of joy, hearts align.
Time stands still, as laughter rings,
In the embrace of simple things.

So let us wander, hand in hand,
Through dreams of paradise, on this land.
With reverence, let us truly see,
The beauty in life, wild and free.

Echoes of Tenderness

In a quiet room, the warmth remains,
Echoes of laughter, soothing the pains.
Soft whispers linger, like a sweet song,
Binding our hearts where we belong.

Raindrops tap on the windowpane,
A gentle rhythm, like love's refrain.
We find connection in every tear,
In the embrace of those we hold dear.

Time weaves moments, cherished and frail,
Every heartbeat tells a tale.
In solitude's arms, we find our peace,
A tender love that will never cease.

Golden sunlight streams through the haze,
Illuminating our darkest days.
With every breath, we learn to feel,
The echoes of love that softly heal.

Together we rise, hand in hand,
Facing the world, a united stand.
In the fabric of life, we weave our thread,
With echoes of tenderness gently spread.

The Night's Secret

Beneath the stars, a mystery lies,
In the whispered winds and shadowed skies.
Silent secrets the night bestows,
In depths of darkness, true beauty grows.

Moonlight dances on leaves so green,
While fireflies flicker, a shimmering scene.
As dreams take flight on this velvet sea,
The night unveils what's meant to be.

Voices of crickets serenade the dark,
While hearts ignite, an eternal spark.
In the stillness, the world holds its breath,
As we embrace the night's sweet depth.

Time seems to pause in this tranquil space,
With every heartbeat, we find our place.
In the mystery of shadows cast,
The night's secret whispers, deep and vast.

So let us wander beneath the night,
Setting our souls to endless flight.
In the embrace of starlit bliss,
We discover true love in every kiss.

Between the Tick and Tock

In the quiet spaces where moments blend,
Time holds its breath, a faithful friend.
Between the tick and the gentle tock,
Life's precious secrets softly unlock.

A fleeting smile, a glance exchanged,
In every heartbeat, life's rearranged.
We dance through seconds, both fast and slow,
Finding joy in the ebb and flow.

Ticking clocks in the silent night,
Whisper dreams, taking flight.
In the pause, we breathe, we sigh,
Moments cherished, never goodbye.

With every second, stories unfold,
Carved in time, both brave and bold.
We carry wishes, hopes tightly bound,
Between the tick and the tock, we are found.

So let's hold on to these precious hours,
In the garden of time, blooming flowers.
As life rushes by, let's take a pause,
Between the tick and tock, love is our cause.

In the Intervals of Breath

In moments still, we find our peace,
A gentle sigh, the world does cease.
Each heartbeat calls, a whispered thread,
In the intervals, our spirits tread.

With every pause, a thought takes flight,
Shadows dance in soft low light.
Within the silence, wisdom gleams,
Life breathes slow, and so it seems.

The rustling leaves, a fleeting sound,
Nature's pulse, forever bound.
In quietude, our souls align,
In the intervals, the stars will shine.

Time stretches wide, horizons blend,
Moments linger, they don't end.
Hope is born in every breath,
In silence, we embrace what's left.

As twilight falls and dreams arise,
We find solace beneath dark skies.
With every breath, we come alive,
In this space, our spirits thrive.

Temporary Treasures

A fleeting glance, a smile so bright,
Moments shared, pure delight.
Like grains of sand, they slip away,
Temporary, yet here to stay.

In whispered words, we bind our hearts,
Each laugh and tear, a work of art.
Collecting memories like morning dew,
Temporary treasures, shared by two.

Seasons change, the colors fade,
Yet every bond, a fond cascade.
In the blink of an eye, we'll part,
But in the shadows, you hold my heart.

Through hours spent and paths we roam,
Each given moment, a cherished home.
Though transient as the autumn air,
These temporary treasures, ever rare.

In golden light, we take our stand,
Holding tight to what's unplanned.
For in each flicker, love we find,
Temporary treasures, forever bind.

The Art of Disappearing

In the pull of night, I fade away,
A silhouette, lost in the fray.
With gentle steps, I hush my breath,
Dancing close to the edge of death.

Whispers call from shadows near,
Tales of longing, masked in fear.
In every heartbeat, I slip and slide,
The art of disappearing, my silent guide.

With every sunset, I blend in,
Where laughter echoes and sorrows thin.
In the quiet mist, I find my grace,
In spaces lost, I carve my place.

Yet in each flicker, I come alive,
The shifting dusk causes me to thrive.
For art is born from the shades we wear,
Disappearance, a canvas bare.

And as the stars begin to gleam,
In the silence, I chase my dream.
For in vanishing, I may just see,
The beauty found in being free.

Chasing Shadows in the Twilight

In twilight's embrace, shadows grow long,
A dance of light, where we belong.
Every step, a silent chase,
Seeking solace in this space.

Colors blend in the fading day,
Where night comes to softly play.
With whispers low, the stars ignite,
Chasing shadows in the night.

In laughter's echo, memories flow,
As dreams unfurl, like wings they grow.
Underneath the vast sky's dome,
We wander far, we find our home.

Each shadow cast tells tales untold,
Of fleeting moments, brave and bold.
In the twilight glow, we find our way,
Chasing shadows until the day.

For in this dance, we lose and find,
A whispered truth, a tangled mind.
In every flicker, our spirits soar,
Chasing shadows forevermore.

Tidal Waves of Memory

Crashing waves upon the shore,
Whispers of the days before.
Each ripple tells a hidden tale,
Where joy and sorrow gently sail.

Fading footprints in the sand,
Echoes of a time so grand.
Memories in the moon's embrace,
A timeless waltz in a fleeting space.

Waves will come and waves will go,
Yet the heart still aches to know.
Each crest a thought, each trough a sigh,
In the tide, our moments lie.

Battles lost and victories won,
Underneath a setting sun.
The ocean's call is ever near,
Drowning thoughts we hold so dear.

Tidal waves of memory rise,
Holding dreams in watery skies.
From depths of loss to shores of grace,
We find our strength, we find our place.

Conversations in the Void

Silence echoes through the night,
Stars converse with distant light.
Words unspoken fill the air,
Thoughts like shadows linger there.

In the void, we find our peace,
Every heartbeat, a wild release.
Emotions dance in fragile forms,
Where calmness meets the raging storms.

Listen close to what's not said,
Messages in whispers spread.
Between the beats of time and space,
Resides our truth, our sacred place.

Lonely nights and staring skies,
Searching for the unseen ties.
In reflections' depth, we peep,
Words unvoiced that still run deep.

Conversations lost in dreams,
Flow like water, like moonbeams.
In the silence, we are found,
In the void, a sacred sound.

A Dance With Disappearance

Fleeting moments, quiet grace,
A dance we share, a soft embrace.
Fade into the dusk's warm glow,
Where shadows whisper, and time flows.

Twilight dances on the edge,
With every step, a silent pledge.
To capture time, to hold it near,
Yet see it slip, we shed a tear.

In the waltz of joy and pain,
We float like leaves in gentle rain.
Disappearance is part of art,
A fleeting brush, then we depart.

Calmly twirling, round we go,
Rhythm soft, like muted snow.
In every turn, a whisper lost,
In every step, we count the cost.

A dance with night, a kiss with fate,
Embracing both, we celebrate.
For in the dance of loss and gain,
We find our joy, we face the pain.

Unexpected Interludes

A sudden laugh, a fleeting glance,
In quiet moments, life's sweet dance.
A spark ignites, a heart's delight,
Unexpected joy in the fading light.

In whispers shared beneath the stars,
We find our truth, we heal our scars.
A simple smile, an open door,
Moments woven, forever more.

Time stands still in these brief frames,
When life reveals its hidden games.
Serendipity's gentle touch,
Reminding us we've gained so much.

Coffee cups and stories told,
Inside each heart, a world of gold.
Unexpected, yet so profound,
In gentle waves, our dreams are found.

Endings come, yet still we rise,
In every tear, in every sigh.
Embracing all that life can send,
In unexpected interludes, we blend.

Ephemeral Encounters

In a crowded room, eyes briefly meet,
Silent stories in a heartbeat's beat.
Fleeting smiles that softly fade,
Echoes of warmth in moments made.

Hands brush past, a spark ignites,
A shared glance under city lights.
Yet time marches on, shadows creep,
In the night's embrace, memories seep.

A laugh shared, a sigh released,
Words unspoken, yet love increased.
Paths intertwine, just for a while,
Each encounter, a secret smile.

The clock chimes softly; the hour's late,
Tender moments sealed by fate.
In the rearview, reflections blend,
Ephemeral echoes that never end.

Cherished whispers fade into night,
Palms parting, hearts taking flight.
What was once close, now drifts away,
In splendid memory, it forever stays.

Whispers in the Gaps

In the breaths between our words,
Lie the secrets that are heard.
Subtle hints and fleeting sighs,
Lurking thoughts behind closed eyes.

The pauses hold unspoken dreams,
Silent motions filled with themes.
In this quiet, truths can bloom,
Finding light in shadowed room.

Soft footfalls along the shore,
Nature's heart beats evermore.
Waves of whispers, tides of grace,
Moments captured, time's embrace.

In the gaps, we find our voice,
In the silence, we rejoice.
Every glance, a gentle dance,
In the quiet, love's expanse.

Embrace the stillness, breathe it in,
Life's sweet stories now begin.
For in the gaps, we shape our fate,
Whispers binding, hearts create.

Echoing Silences

In the void where laughter fades,
Silence lingers, the heart cascades.
Forgotten echoes softly call,
Through the stillness, shadows fall.

The air is thick with dreams unsaid,
In the hush, our spirits tread.
Each heartbeat a ghost, a trace,
In the silence, we find our space.

Time slows down, a breath is drawn,
In quietude, a new dawn.
Memories linger like a song,
In the silence, we belong.

Words unvoiced paint the skies,
In the stillness, hope never dies.
Whispers around us, intertwining,
Echoing love, forever shining.

Through the silence, we learn to fly,
With every breath, we touch the sky.
In echoed stillness, we'll remain,
Hearts connected, joy and pain.

Moments Like Fading Sand

Time drips slowly through our hands,
Each second slips, like sinking sands.
Memories fade, yet linger near,
In every laugh and whispered cheer.

Golden glimmers of a past embrace,
Softly washing upon our grace.
Fleeting shadows dance in light,
Moments captured vanish from sight.

A desert breeze, a quiet sigh,
In every tear, a chance to fly.
Like grains of sand, we ebb and flow,
Carved by time, forever aglow.

In the hourglass, life's sweet chase,
Moments merge, then leave no trace.
Yet in our hearts, they'll ever stay,
Guiding us along the way.

Fading, shimmering, they pass each day,
In this journey, come what may.
For every moment, whether grand or bland,
Is a treasure, like fading sand.

Shadows of Embrace

In twilight, whispers breathe soft,
Beneath the veil, where dreams aloft.
Fingers entwined, we sway as one,
Chasing the light, till day is done.

The night unfolds with secrets deep,
In tender arms, where shadows creep.
A hush of hope in silent vows,
We dance as if, time slows the hours.

Horizon bleeds a crimson hue,
Embracing all we thought we knew.
Each heartbeat a sonnet unchained,
In shadows' depth, love's joy remained.

Memories flicker like candle flames,
Echoes of laughter, soft, sweet names.
In the stillness, our spirits soar,
Shadows of embrace, forevermore.

The moonlight wraps us, a gentle shroud,
In whispered dreams, we are unbowed.
Together in this tranquil night,
Our shadows blend, lost in the light.

Threads of a Vanished Hour

Time slips away like grains of sand,
Moments unfurling, unplanned strands.
In the tapestry, colors fade,
Fleeting whispers of choices made.

Each stitch a memory we weave tight,
In the quiet, a flicker of light.
Yet threads unravel, softly frayed,
A daydream's end in twilight laid.

Laughter dances on the breeze,
Echoing softly among the trees.
We grasp at dreams, like fireflies,
As twilight blooms, a soft goodbye.

In the labyrinth of ticking hands,
We chase the echoes, distant lands.
Each hour transformed, a fleeting art,
Threads of life stitched into the heart.

Now the hourglass stands still and pure,
Holding shadows that we endure.
In silence, find what remains dear,
Threads of a vanished hour, clear.

Chasing the Unseen

In the glimmer of dawn's first light,
I chase the unseen, out of sight.
Echoes of dreams like whispers call,
Risking the fall, I dare it all.

A shadow dances on the wall,
Tempting my heart to rise, to sprawl.
In every heartbeat, a hidden spark,
Guiding me forth, igniting the dark.

Through tangled paths where hope resides,
I follow the rhythm where truth hides.
Each step a promise, quietly sown,
Chasing the unseen, seeds are grown.

As dusk unfolds, the night draws near,
In veils of stars, I shed my fear.
With every breath, I seek and yearn,
Chasing the unseen, I shall return.

The horizon whispers tales of flair,
In every corner of the air.
Though unseen paths may twist and wind,
My heart, relentless, love defined.

Glimpses of Laughter

In sunlit fields, the laughter swells,
Echoing sweetly, happiness dwells.
Every giggle a fleeting chase,
Moments of joy in a tender place.

Through sunshine's lens, we play and spin,
Capturing joy that lies within.
A tickle here, a game of pretend,
In glances shared, we find our blend.

Underneath the wide blue sky,
Hearts unfurl as the birds fly high.
Each glance exchanged, a silent cheer,
Glimpses of laughter, very near.

Amidst the chaos, joy is found,
In the simplest things that come around.
With every chuckle and radiant beam,
We weave a tapestry, love's sweet dream.

In this laughter, let time freeze,
Memories linger like a gentle breeze.
For in those moments, dreams ignite,
Glimpses of laughter, pure delight.

Melodies of the Unremembered

Whispers of dawn in the silent air,
Forgotten songs that float with care.
Notes of dreams, gently entwined,
Echoes of moments left behind.

Time dances softly, a fleeting bead,
Each melody whispers, sows a seed.
Vibrations linger, both old and new,
Crafting a symphony, tender and true.

In shadowed corners, the heart will sing,
To the tune of what the past may bring.
With every note, a story unfolds,
Of love, of loss, in silence retold.

Resounding truths in the quiet night,
Carried on whispers, shadows take flight.
Guardians of sorrows, joy interlaced,
Melodies binding the lost with grace.

Through the veil of time, the echoes play,
Crafting a dreamscape, a soft array.
A dance with the unremembered we share,
In the heart's deep chamber, lingering there.

Where Time Lingers

In hush of twilight, moments freeze,
Beneath the stars, we find our ease.
Time stretches thin, a silken thread,
Where whispers collide, and dreams are fed.

Memory holds, a tender embrace,
Each heartbeat a step, each step a trace.
In the stillness, our spirits soar,
Navigating paths we long to explore.

Ephemeral sands slip through our hands,
Yet in this stillness, our heart understands.
Where laughter resides, and shadows play,
Time lingers softly, never to stray.

A canvas vast with colors bright,
Brush strokes of moments, pure delight.
In the gallery of life, we roam,
Finding our solace, our crafted home.

As dawn breaks forth, the echoes fade,
Yet still we linger, unafraid.
In the light of memory, love is found,
Where time stands still, our hearts are bound.

The Essence of Now

In the stillness, the world unwinds,
A moment captured, where truth aligns.
Breath of the present, so sweet, so clear,
In the essence of now, we find our cheer.

Fleeting shadows dance on walls,
Carrying stories of whispered calls.
Life's gentle current, a shimmering flow,
In the embrace of now, we learn to grow.

Emotions awaken, vibrant and bright,
Every glance holds the weight of light.
In the quiet beats of the heart's own song,
We discover the place where we truly belong.

Through laughter and tears, we weave the thread,
In the fabric of moments, where dreams are fed.
Celebrating now, we cherish the gift,
In the folds of existence, our spirits uplift.

Letting go of the chains of the past,
In the essence of now, our shadows cast.
With open hearts, we embrace the day,
Finding joy in the dance, come what may.

Brushstrokes of a Memory

In colors bright and shades of blue,
A memory painted, vivid and true.
Each stroke a story, a laugh, a tear,
Canvas of moments we hold so dear.

With every hue, emotions blend,
Whispered secrets that time won't end.
In the gallery of our heart, we see,
A portrait of lives lived wild and free.

Textures of life, both smooth and rough,
Crafting a tapestry, rich and tough.
In shadows cast, our fears find release,
Brushstrokes of memory, capturing peace.

Fragments of joy and the echoes of pain,
Illuminate paths like after the rain.
Each moment lingers, a vibrant plea,
In the art of living, we find our key.

A brush in hand, we color the void,
With light and shadow, sorrows alloyed.
In the heart's soft canvas, forever we trace,
Our memories etched, in time and grace.

At sunset's glow, as colors fade,
We cherish the strokes, the love portrayed.
With every breath, we blend and define,
The brushstrokes of memory, forever divine.

Glimpses of the Unheld

In shadows where dreams might dwell,
A whisper of warmth, a silent bell.
Fleeting moments, golden and rare,
Stories untold linger in the air.

Fingers reach for what slips away,
Echoes of laughter in soft ballet.
Fragments of joy, like stars that we chase,
Caught in the light of a fleeting grace.

Time dances lightly on petals of dew,
Glimmers of hope in every hue.
A tapestry woven with threads of the past,
Each heartbeat a memory woven to last.

In twilight's embrace, we softly sigh,
As shadows stretch long beneath the sky.
The unheld moments, the wishes unsent,
Bring solace to hearts that lightly lament.

In the stillness, we gather the dreams,
In the quiet, the soft memory beams.
Through glimpses of life, we learn to believe,
In love's gentle echoes, we truly receive.

Fading Footsteps

In the dust of paths once explored,
Footsteps fade, memories adored.
Silent echoes whisper our name,
Time's gentle hand plays its game.

Leaves tumble down, scattered and free,
Each rustle a note in nature's decree.
Sunset drapes over the weary road,
While shadows of yesterday softly erode.

Winds carry tales of journeys long gone,
Footfalls in rhythm, a fading song.
The heart feels the weight of what cannot stay,
As daylight dims and turns to grey.

But in the silence, we still find a way,
To cherish the moments, come what may.
Though footsteps may fade into the night,
Their presence lingers, a guiding light.

In the tapestry of time, we weave,
Every step a gift, something to believe.
Even as we part, love remains,
In the tapestry of life, joy remains.

The Lullaby of Lost Hours

When twilight hums its gentle tune,
The moon whispers secrets to the dune.
Hours slip by like grains of sand,
In restless dreams, we take a stand.

Stars blink softly in their distant dance,
While time weaves shadows in a trance.
Melodies linger on soft, sweet breath,
In the lullaby of life, whispers of death.

Where fleeting moments flow like rivers wide,
Lost hours dwell, our hearts as guide.
With every sigh, we touch the night,
Searching for solace in soft twilight.

Crickets sing of solace unknown,
In a world where the weary have grown.
Under the canopy of a velvet sky,
We cradle our dreams, watch time slip by.

For in the silence, our hearts may find,
The lullabies of the lost, intertwined.
As we drift past the hours that fade,
In the cradle of time, our worries laid.

Surreal Seconds

Seconds slip by, a painted dream,
In the fabric of now, life's gentle seam.
Moments stretch, then swiftly rewind,
Reality danced with the curious mind.

In vibrant hues, time's canvas unfolds,
Whispers of wonders, secrets untold.
Mirrors reflect what we cannot see,
The essence of life, the heart's melody.

Clouds drift lazily across the blue,
Each one a thought, fleeting and true.
With every blink, a story is spun,
Under the gaze of the hiding sun.

Surreal seconds, a kaleidoscope view,
Where dreams blend with what's strikingly new.
A carousel spins, colors collide,
In the heart of the moment, time cannot hide.

So we gather the fragments and lift them high,
With laughter and love, we dare to fly.
In the surreal dance of unforgettable sights,
We find our voices in starlit nights.

www.ingramcontent.com/pod-product-compliance
Ingram Content Group UK Ltd.
Pitfield, Milton Keynes, MK11 3LW, UK
UKHW041839141224
452457UK00012B/527